What a Morning!

What a Morning!

The Christmas Story in Black Spirituals

Selected and edited by John Langstaff
Illustrated by Ashley Bryan
Arrangements for singing and piano by John Andrew Ross

Aladdin Paperbacks

For Debby
a woman of integrity, vision and determination

—J. L.

To the memory of my aunt
Hilda Bryan Mowatt

—A. B.

A "NOTE TO TEACHERS, PARENTS AND INSTRUMENTALISTS"
APPEARS ON THE FINAL PAGE OF THIS BOOK.

First Aladdin Paperbacks edition October 1996
Text copyright © 1987 by John Langstaff
Illustrations copyright © 1987 by Ashley Bryan
Musical arrangements copyright © 1987 by John Andrew Ross

Aladdin Paperbacks
An imprint of Simon & Schuster
Children's Publishing Division
1230 Avenue of the Americas
New York, NY 10020

Also available in a Simon & Schuster Books for Young Readers edition
Printed and bound in Hong Kong

10   9   8   7   6   5   4   3   2   1

The Library of Congress has cataloged the hardcover edition as follows:
What a morning!
Summary: Five illustrated spirituals dealing with the birth of Christ
on the first Christmas morning.
Includes printed music for voice and piano.
1. Spirituals (Songs)—Juvenile.   2. Christmas music—Juvenile.
[1. Jesus Christ—Nativity—Songs and music.
2. Spirituals (Songs).   3. Christmas music]   I. Langstaff, John M.
II. Bryan, Ashley, ill.
M1670.W48   1987   87-750130
ISBN 0-689-50422-5

ISBN 0-689-80807-0 (Aladdin pbk.)

The original pictures for *What a Morning!*
The Christmas Story in Black Spirituals are tempera paintings.

And I will give him the morning star....
—REVELATIONS II: 28

Be watchful, and strengthen the things which remain....
—REVELATIONS III: 2

MY LORD WHAT A MORNING!

For unto us a child is born, unto us a son is given;
and his name shall be called Wonderful, Counselor, the Prince of Peace.

—ISAIAH IX: 6

My Lord, What a Morning!

MARY HAD A BABY

And she brought forth her firstborn son,
and wrapped him in swaddling clothes,
and laid him in a manger.

—LUKE II: 7

Mary Had a Baby

GO, TELL IT ON THE MOUNTAIN

And there were in the same country shepherds abiding in the field, keeping watch over their flock by night.
And suddenly there was a multitude of the heavenly host praising God, and saying, ...

—LUKE II: 8

Go, Tell It on the Mountain

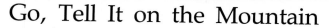

Slow, with a deliberate pulse ♩.=76

Go, tell it on the moun - tain, O - ver the hills and ev'-ry - where.

Go, tell it on the moun - tain that Je - sus Christ is

Fine

born! _____

1.While shep - herds kept their watch - ing O'er
2. The shep - herds feared and trem - bled, When
3. An an - gel came from glo - ry, To

si - lent flocks by night, Be - hold, through-out the _____
lo! a - bove the earth Rang out the an - gel _____
hail the Sav - ior's birth, And then a light from _____

hea - ven there shone a ho - ly light. _____
cho - rus that hailed our Je - sus' birth. _____
hea - ven shone on the ho - ly place. _____

D.C. al Fine

Sister Mary Had-a But One Child

Gentle, but with rhythmic motion ♩=60

Capo V

Lyrics:

Sis-ter Ma-ry had-a but one child, Born in Beth-le-hem; An'-a

ev-e-ry time the lit-tle ba-by cried, she rocked him in a wea-ry land.

She rocked him in a wea-ry land. Oh, land.

Verse

Three Wise Men from Je-ru-sa-lem came, they tra-vell'd ve-ry far.

They said, "Where is He born King of the Jews? For we have seen His

star, for we have seen His star." Sis-ter

D.S. al Fine

BEHOLD THAT STAR!

And lo, the star, which they saw in the east,
went before them, till it came and stood over
where the young child was.

—MATTHEW II: 9

Behold That Star!

Note to Teachers, Parents and Instrumentalists

Black spirituals have a particularly powerful impact through their splendid melodies ("Go, Tell It on the Mountain"), free rhythmic flow of natural declamation ("Sister Mary Had-a But One Child"), and texts of poetic imagery ("My Lord, What a Morning!"). Together, these elements create a strikingly beautiful art form, not only a great expression of African-American heritage, but an eloquent expression for all people today.

Feeling about these songs as I do, I have selected a few spirituals to illumine the Christmas story with the rich diversity of this music, from a mother's simple lullaby to an angel's clarion declaration. Other spirituals narrate the story of the shepherds, the kings, the family and "the star"—the early-morning star, the star that lit the manger at midnight, the star that guided foreign peoples to the stable. It is important that we have a book for children, stemming from this great heritage of music, used in context with the inspiring story of the Nativity and portrayed pictorially by an outstanding Black artist.

As with most folk music, spirituals are effectively sung without any accompaniment. In the piano settings here, the melody is in the top line of the piano or organ part (when it is not written as a separate vocal line), but the other lines of the setting can be sung or hummed as choral accompaniment to the melody. (Occasionally, optional notes for singing or playing are printed in smaller type.) Call and response can be a distinctive part of many of these songs, as a lead singer lines out the verses, with the chorus joining in. Singers can be encouraged to make up additional verses as the song progresses ("Mary Had a Baby": *Angels sang around him....Who heard the singing?...Shepherds heard the singing....Star kept a-shining....*).

The suggested harmonies for the guitar chords may not always fit the chords of the piano accompaniment. For those less-experienced guitarists, we have suggested the use of the capo to get the same effect: attach the capo on the second or fifth fret as noted at the bottom of the music, and then play the chords indicated in parentheses.

John Langstaff
Christmas 1987